Hands Reaching in Water

Hands Reaching in Water

Gary Hyland

Hagios Press
Box 33024 Cathedral PO
Regina SK S4T 7X2

Copyright © 2007 Gary Hyland

All rights reserved. No part of this publication may be reproduced, stored in a retrieval system, or transmitted in any form or by any means without the prior written permission of the publisher or by licensed agreement with Access: The Canadian Copyright Licensing Agency. Exceptions will be made in the case of a reviewer, who may quote brief passages in a review to print in a magazine or newspaper, broadcast on radio or television, or post on the Internet.

Library and Archives Canada Cataloguing in Publication

Hyland, Gary, 1940-
   Hands reaching in water / Gary Hyland.

Poems.
ISBN 978-0-9739727-6-4

  I. Title.
PS8565.Y53H35 2007   C811'.54   C2007-901825-4

Edited by Paul Wilson.
Designed and typeset by Donald Ward.
Cover painting: *Blue Trapeze* by Bill Bragg, oil on canvas, 68" x 48"
   (artist represented by the Art Ark Gallery, Kelowna, BC,
   www.LookatArt.com/Bragg).
Cover design by Yves Noblet.
Set in ITC Galliard.
Printed and bound in Canada at Houghton Boston Printers & Lithographers, Saskatoon.

The publishers gratefully acknowledge the assistance of the Saskatchewan Arts Board, The Canada Council for the Arts, and the Cultural Industries Development Fund (Saskatchewan Department of Culture, Youth & Recreation) in the production of this book.

for Sister Ida Marie Grenon
inspiring teacher of high school English

Contents

HAMMEL

How Hammel Flew Upstairs	10
Voodoo State	11
Remote Control	12
George?	14
Hammel Looking	16
In the Pelting Rain	17
Not Today	19
That Loving Feeling	21
Hammel's Lament	22
Hammel Bugged	23
Hammel's George Sanders Disease	24
His Dodge	25
Hammel at Buffalo Lake	26
Landing	27
Hammel Attempts Sleep	28
His Truest Friend	30
Yawn	32
As Naked as It Gets: Twenty-Five Notes for an Unwritten Essay	33

HIT AND RUNS

It Could Have Been	42
Or Say	44
Grape	46
Discussion Late at Night	48
Vortal Tomb, Poulnabrone	50
Ravel in Automobile Accident	58
Mildly Manic: A Poet Meets John Nash in McLean Hospital, Boston, 1959	59
Hit and Runs	67

MOTIVES FOR BEAUTY

Motives for Beauty	74
Dream Place	76
Crime Sites	77
Last Quarter Man	78
Woman After Woman	79
Guys from Here	80
The Illusion of Going Forward	84
Star of [insert name of once-popular TV show] Dies	85
Alternate Cancer Therapy	87
Starting Lines	88
Shock	90
Reach	91

STAKES IN THE RIVER

A Brief History of Zero	94
Infinity's Twin	98
Miami Holiday	99
Vision: Foot Descending	100
Interviewees, Sept. 11, 2001	102
Hudson River Breezes	103
We Kill Well	104
Borden and Morris in 2104	106
Stakes in the River	108
By the Fifteenth Cosmological Decade	110

HANDS REACHING IN WATER

Heroes in Coffins	114
The Fragile Things	115
Hands Reaching in Water *or* The Short Rule of the Philosopher-Kings	116
Arguments in the Garden of Prayer	119
Notes	133
Acknowledgements	135

HAMMEL

HOW HAMMEL FLEW UPSTAIRS

Something from inside him
precedes him up the stairs
something vaporous
too small, too capricious
to be a guardian angel.

And certainly not a wish
or dream made palpable
by ardent tremors
of urgency luring him
skyward with a promise,

whatever that might be.
Creating a lightness
in the heart of his stomach
it slips out erratically
and wings a flight or two.

Ho-hum. More exuberance.
Another extrusion of ecstasy
and him with no excuse,
no ingested sparkle, no up-
lifting lore, revelation, tryst.

Just this cheek-bursting grin,
this eye-creasing galumphy
grin, declaring to any
who surprise him: harmless
but irretrievably raptured.

Gary Hyland

VOODOO STATE

A jab of hate wakes him while others sleep.
A voodoo state from memory cuts
with replayed clips that shred his guts.
How can she close her eyes in peace
Who burned an hour past beneath
Another's hands? Such inequity
Incenses Hammel. The Greeks likely
Hatched a god whose job it is to prod
His brain with living-colour cuckoldry
And inject his heart with misery.
Whoever claimed rainfall in the brain
Left the body dry was a well-slept clod.
Not tears, but this flooded inner plain
Washes him from slumber into pain.

REMOTE CONTROL

Hammel has fallen asleep peering through the picture window of an image by his friend The Poet. He wakes to the TV spouting news of Diego Cardaenza who has strapped explosives to his lover's body. Via cell phone while hovering over a laptop in his van, Diego threatens to detonate her and the neighborhood. His terrified lover, Suzette, in view of him and the world, trembles on the balcony of her flat, cell phone to her ear, her building and those nearby evacuated. Helicopters whacking the air. Comely media commentators lathering over the tactics of terrorism applied to a personal crisis. The special ops brass, cells pressed to their ears, consult with psychiatrists and hostage specialists. Snipers and demolition experts consider how to take him out in less than a pulse.

A commentator deadpans, "Science and technology make this moment possible." Hammel is horrified and deeply empathetic. His attention wanders to what would have happened if he had his ex wired thus. Or vice versa. The temptations of remote control.

Something dark outside his window startles Diego. A cell phone on a cable. Diego takes it inside, puts it to his free ear. He explains to the police that he will not blow half their city to microspecks but, instead, just neatly dispose of Suzette, if they will agree to charge him jointly with her murder and that of the fetus she carries. "Now we know what kinda nutto we got," says one of the cops.

Gary Hyland

A detective's voice tells Diego the cell phone could have been a bomb that left him headless. Diego tells the policeman that would have automatically blown up Suzette and most of downtown since his van is trigger-packed with liquid nitrogen. The detective asks him if he is hungry. He says he has lots of food and cigarettes. Suzette wants an abortion? He'll give her an abortion. He'll de-womb the whole damn city.

Hammel's phone rings. His friend The Poet wants some routine information. She knows nothing of Diego. "In the garden all day," she says, "tending sparse and prickly things that may well be weeds, watching bees turn into angels and back again, making notes." So he tells her all of it, the story of Suzette and Diego, the fetus and the police and the reporters and commentators on all the channels. He speculates on the many who have called in sick or returned from work and are now ordering pizzas so they will be watching when whatever is going to happen happens.

The Poet thanks him and says she is returning to the garden to watch the bees and the stars becoming leaves on her late April trees.

And there he is, alone with Diego and Suzette, growing uncomfortable watching himself watch them. So he goes to the window. It is the time of day when the shrubs lay down shadows longer than themselves. Something moves, almost hovers, near the lilacs. It may not be an angel but he hopes it is.

GEORGE?

When Hammel gets this sludged on medication and scotch he sometimes recalls that he had a son but did he really or is this another erasure the doctor will say he has to make, a slice of reality too thin for his sandwich, after all no one has been coming around saying how's it going, Dad, or sending birthday cards, which might have been nice now and then especially on those evenings when he was going to kill himself and thus out of these blurred non-reveries George, named for Hammel's father, emerges, a young man now mid-thirtyish living in a semi-tropical Asian place so that he only gets home on occasion appearing out-of-the-blue like Willy Loman's brother Ben and working at something so completely needing all his life he himself is unpartnered, yet he is perceptive and sensitive and so swollen with memory he can give Hammel transfusions from the past like the time they went back to the old farmstead and Hammel found in the basement ruins of the ancestral shack a wrinkly picture of his grandfather and his mother and from her smile Hammel had concluded that there was at least one time she wasn't slagged by life but whatever became of that picture, corroboration of George's existence, or did it also maybe not exist, which is when, confused and hopeful, he forces himself into the old family album and that is where, George fading like a wisp, he finds the list he had also forgotten even though he had made it at least within the last few years, and at first he can't remember why the names are there immortalized in what he thinks is chronological order, two old school chums, the guy who used to be his best friend, and five women, all of whom had said they loved him and now didn't or couldn't, a sad scorecard, though he was sure his very Hammelness had closed those portals, that particular combination of indistinction and shallow profundity that induced major ho-humness even in George his own flash and brood, now almost a vapour as at last at last at last Hammel starts to drift into one of his approximations of sleep.

HAMMEL LOOKING

Hammel looking all his life to change
his life — burning bushes; grotto visions;
a poet resurrected singing strange
verses with quickening revelations.
An enchantress who will illuminate
the four tensions that wring him apart
simultaneously yet not dominate
his being. The stories, the plays, the art,
the music, the dance that could restore
the excitement they used to impart.
After Blake, Rilke, Yeats and scotch galore
demolished his brain, not much surprises him.
The fireworks of poems in time grow dim.
Even those he kindled have become a bore.

Gary Hyland

IN THE PELTING RAIN

When he finds himself holding on to the edge of night for life whether it's dear or not Hammel reminds himself that many of the snugly burghers snoozing in their cozy chambers while he slops past in the pelting rain are just one flick of fate from his what is it predicament circumstance impasse mess and the eaves is plenty wide enough though most would choose some less obvious means of self-erasure than scotch and water and walking around in the pelting rain or maybe feel less sorry for themselves and believe as he once believed that coping mechanisms can inhale a blob of loneliness and exhale decorative cumulus splendor well good luck because this thing is more like some Magellanic cloud of endless space crapola that never stops and over time craters your ego and your guts because after the dating services the public speaking class the internet chat disasters the social dancing classes the inter-faith bible study group the singles bars the singles clubs the yoga class the diets the new wardrobes the exercise programs the hair restoratives the counseling and yes yes yes the pills and creams guaranteed to enlarge his penis there is a tendency to become a smidge discouraged as who would not hope being perhaps eternal but after such a dark torrent not resilient enough to spring in the human breast so much as repine in a sogginess inside his well-drenched Fruit of the Looms and Hammel imagines Craig Pierce whose offices fill a floor in the building he has just now entered to escape the pelting rain and who at one time suggested Hammel lease a life Craig's middle-age spread spreading his wife on whom he depends far more than he knows departed his anxieties biting into his business his scalp coming out to play his counter measures one by one not counting and Hammel is more than consoled he wears resplendently his lopsy smile sitting on the stairs of Craig Pierce's office building at 4 a.m. his clothes on the bannister as the cleaning lady enters.

NOT TODAY

Another day he didn't die
and Hammel leaks gratitude
in the general direction of
a divine beneficence.

Not being dead is the best way
to enjoy life's antidotes —
TV, books and movies,
traffic-free late-night drives.

The storm outside would freeze
his blood before he sneezed,
but natural gas, insulation,
wood and wool save his life.

So now, alone in the house,
he sings his awful version
of "Wonderful, Wonderful"
and waltzes with his winter coat.

He sings himself a wondrous life
of warm, concocted memories
a sweet and tender paradise
of Hammel-centred love

that might have been love
had he not been Hammel —
a crazy, crazy moon-crazed bat
he sings and drops in a chair.

*Failure's the only thing you've
not failed at.* Whereupon
he laughs his laugh and declares
he's earned another scotch.

THAT LOVING FEELING

3:30 a.m. and Hammel is driving up and down the streets in his beige '84 Dodge with the bumper sticker that reads Pardon me for driving too close in front of you, following the same route like a bus driver which causes the cops to pull him over with siren and spastic lights and try to match him to one of the night's felonies but his priors have expired, he's off alcohol and his pills don't register on their instruments, so he goes "scotch free" as he chuckles it to himself, but then the golden oldies station is telling him once again that he has lost that loving feeling and he's trying to remember when last he had it and where he might have put it, but he can't even conjure a reasonable description, names being all that float to the surface of his alphabet soup: Joan, the very first to say she loved him and three years ago at the reunion let on she didn't know him; Sherri who took three weeks to angle through him to nail his friend; Charmaine, radiant, radiant Charmaine who after school stepped into a well of mystery; Mavis whom he married and who faded faster than a crocus; Marna who suffered forth a brief facsimile of love, not much to swell on there and no one who might have high-tailed with his loving feeling, which leads him to conjecture he may never have had it or if he did may not have known it from his usual foggy brew, his asthma or insomnia. So was that a loving feeling the times Mavis cried and he asked what was wrong and she said, "Nothing," and he believed her, or was it his wanting to chain her bartender boyfriend to a cement mixer and run it into the river, or maybe it's the way he is beginning to feel about the forty-ish, plumpish redhead in the 7-11 who nods his way when he drives slowly by every thirty minutes wearing his newly-developed sensitive-guy-needing-love look?

HAMMEL'S LAMENT

At the end of the trail there's not enough you
left. How're you gonna be all the things
you still have to be and want to be
when you're always running out of yourself?

It leaks out like lubricant from a faulty
valve under too much pressure, the gasket
shot, whatever it might be, the you thing,
it leaks out and you don't know where you are.

It's the same way your body mutinies.
Hair jumps overboard, muscles walk
the plank, a slag of jowls droops on deck
until who's this gimp in the captain's mirror?

Then one night this stranger dies in his sleep
and in the morning you discover it's you.

Gary Hyland

HAMMEL BUGGED

Sow bugs, centipedes, spiders, ants,
more each week, infiltrate
his basement, parade the carpets
and file between his file cabinets,
his shelves of LPs and tapes,
the furnishings left by his mother.
Schools of silverfish infest his books.

Sprays, powders, traps just delay
the invasion. His old back aches
with stooping for them. Carpet beetles
feign death before they're crushed in Kleenex.
Crickets are brittle, crackle like pretzels.
Day after day they penetrate his space
as if, as if, he thinks, in grim rehearsal.

HAMMEL'S GEORGE SANDERS DISEASE

I've been wrinkling so long I'm half past dead.
Soon as he speaks those words they seem old hat,
something someone worth quoting might have said
with others requoting ever after that.
The jokes, the notes, the phone calls, the pleas
even the emergencies are like LPs,
warped ones much over-played, turned scratchy,
victims of the sterile technologies.
Let's face it, he says to himself, this ennui's
a symptom of George Sanders disease.
It may well be time to follow old George
who declared the world impossibly dull
and pulled the pin. If only he could forge
some novel way to convert one to null.

Gary Hyland

HIS DODGE

The car takes Hammel beyond his intentions.
This morning beside a field of flax in bloom
turning sullen blue in the pre-sun sky
was yesterday's trip to the pharmacy.
Now he is out of gas, out of road.
He has turned the wrong way so many times
chasing country music into darkness
he judges he's a few miles south of Sorrow
near Hopeless. The light tells him he's east of home.
His heart tells him home is just a song
in the night. His Dodge slants into the ditch,
locked in reverse, its mirror full of regrets.
His rifle leans against the far door.
Soon a voice will bring directions.

HAMMEL AT BUFFALO LAKE

The wind makes hoodoos of the snow along the shore
then shrieks into the trees and thrashes in bushes.
But this desire is not for those. It is a desire for desiring,
for what once made him unable to ease into completion.

That desire is gone. He could live here in a small shelter,
eat rabbits, berries, fish. Huddle in rampaging weather,
slumber long into the morning and move through the same
day every day, attending to appetites, carving whims.

From the other side of the sky he hears the pale song of the
    sun,
its longing to reclaim the lake, the land, the empty spaces.
Its yearning for him. When he wanted this place. When he
    wanted
the sky, the sun, its nuances playing upon the clouds.

His yearning is for when he would wake early full of longing
and move to it without urgency like a dancer dancing alone.
This is the last desire. What are the wild rose thickets,
a crocus shy in the April grass, if sleep is the only craving?

Must all the passions end, abraded by grains of opposition,
muted by the dust of indifference, the cloak of custom,
their nimble rush numb? The way the wind-scoured ice makes
an end of waves, reaching darkly toward the bottom of the
    lake.

Gone, in spite of prayers against a servile peace, gone
like the herds that ghost the plains and give this place its name.
The trees are filling with shadows. Is beauty diminished without
desire? Or does it remain a consolation? Soon, he will know.

Gary Hyland

LANDING

Like Thales inventing philosophy, Hammel moves unaware precisely where his feet are, his stomach having evolved a stomach, the belt looping below like a drunken smile, and he wonders if this will be one of those times he gets somewhere and returns without something, but half way up the stairs he forgets where that somewhere is because his mind is benumbed by the sudden intrusive thought that he is someone-not-admired-by-anyone, there being no offspring with such natural inclination and no one who visits his basement of file cabinets and boxes full of newspaper and magazine clippings, chronologically and alphabetically arranged by publication and topically indexed and cross-referenced, to utter wows and holy smokes at almost all the spare time of his life consumed with arranging all the information anyone might want from Acupuncture to Zen, a legacy from thirty-two years as a corporate file clerk before computers vaporized everything like his memory of the errand he was on now completely wiped from a brain with a growth cycle inversely related to that of his waistline, a brain where once circuitry sizzled with all the pre-Socratics, the Kennedy assassinations, the Persian hegemony, the Viet Nam War, and his other specialties, the nature of sleep, the penalties of beauty, the indeterminacy of time and the variability of human love, so that he stops in mid-step and ponders the futility of being neither up nor down in a universe where both seem equally unappealing, when suddenly it occurs to him that not even he really cares and were he to assemble enough of life's necessities he could live here on the landing until he died between his bed above and his collections below and that would be entirely appropriate, though on the discovery of his body there would be no one to declare it so.

HAMMEL ATTEMPTS SLEEP

He climbs into the bed where he expects to die,
Old Hammel who never made a stick's worth of
trouble and for whom no one is likely to cry
since he failed with great frequency at love.

Old Hammel, who never made a stick's worth of
trouble except his own which he made double
since he failed with great frequency at love,
tried all his life and seldom rose above rubble.

Trouble, except his own which he made double,
other men managed far more deftly while he
tried all his life and seldom rose above rubble
Contacts! said a sage *will assure supremacy.*

Other men managed far more deftly, while he,
working as hard as he could, was submediocre.
Contacts! said a sage *will assure supremacy.*
When once he found a princess his kiss never woke her.

Working as hard as he could, was submediocre
in all he pursued — that's what life brought him.
When once he found a princess his kiss never woke her.
The first woman who showed an interest got him.

In all he pursued — that's what life brought him —
one relationship that never found a focus
The first woman who showed an interest got him
and her love shriveled faster than a crocus.

Gary Hyland

One relationship that never found a focus.
Hammel, who knew it wasn't his doing only
and her love shriveled faster than a crocus,
now finds himself a year beyond lonely.

Hammel, who knew it wasn't fate bringing only
trouble and for whom no one is likely to cry,
now finds himself a year beyond lonely.
He climbs into the bed where he expects to die.

HIS TRUEST FRIEND

Hammel has an illness with no name.
Once they called it melancholy.

His eyes are dry and red and sunken,
his grabbers tremble in his pockets.

Death wants to kiss his crusted lips as if
she loved him alone and always had.

Long ago he spurned her black mirror,
dismissed her dark good cheer. He should

have solved riddles of vagrant sums.
Instead he tortured puny ambiguities,

while his blood congealed with ironies.
He might have left intact, a sorcerer,

his last act a dive through fire, his last
words a revelation, his last embrace

his life entire. Now he coughs and scowls
and drinks too much and mumbles

to himself in public places, and forgets
to brush his teeth and wipe his ass.

She stays with him, death, through it
all. She'll kiss his broken blisters yet.

Gary Hyland

Your death never lies to you. She will
place her hand where it hurts and say,

"This agony will cease. This tribulation
end." Death, your truest friend, will come

any time you want, sit long nights at
your bedside, never tire, never glance

at the clock. Death will be whichever
sex you require or none at all, so long

as your expectations are complete.
She will be clad as you might imagine

and do swiftly what must be done, no fuss,
unless you should desire one. She will

work in the circumstances you supply:
geriatric cell, living room or vehicle.

She will hang a mirror of bright mica
only you can see, a black liquid face

your face hovers in, and you can look
there any time and see if where you are

is where you should be, for your death
is the measure of your place today.

Hammel, when at last those lips pressed
his, shivered once and groaned, "Shit."

YAWN

You are tired of Hammel,
his nothing-piled-on-nothing
so-called life, his zeroness.

His trivial ups and measly downs
like looking out the car window
from Winnipeg to Calgary.

It's not your fault. The fatigue
of gray on gray. Besides, even
Hammel is tired of Hammel.

He knows he should conclude
and has dreamed the means
and penned departure notes.

This Prufrockian Nowhere Man
is not new and should don
a noose, step off a chair.

Maybe he did. Maybe beneath
his stairs he dangles right now
all that nothing gone at last,

those days of ho and hum
erased, his final breath
an eye-scrunching yawn.

Gary Hyland

AS NAKED AS IT GETS:
TWENTY-FIVE NOTES FOR AN UNWRITTEN ESSAY

1. Kreuzer's verified text of the note Hammel left the server:

   I don't know your name. In any case, you won't long be waiting on tables here or anywhere. You are one of the most attractive women I have ever seen. It gives me great pleasure to watch you. Don't panic, I'm the most meek of creatures and soon to depart. You are elegant and graceful. Your long, slender neck might be the stem of an Etruscan goblet. Your creamy complexion and flaxen hair complement each other. You glow. You may be slightly too narrow in the hips yet your waist is even slimmer. Your legs are long, thin, shapely. Your smile, radiant. Your bearing is natural, revealing supple grace. You might want to correct your habit of walking about with your mouth half open; it's sensual but it detracts from your natural elegance. Merely physical attributes are fine but so impermanent. They can actually be an impediment to the development of a strong, resourceful personality. (See Merriman's *The Expense of Beauty*.) Unless you have developed or are developing an equally appealing inner life, in short a beautiful soul, the odds are not great that you will find much more than shallow, transitory happiness. For you, I wish what I have never found — joy frequent & sustained."

   In Kreuzer's account, there is no mention of a reaction or response from the server. "Hammel: a Life Examined, Part 2"; Wilhelm Kreuzer; *Annals of the American Social Psychology Association*; vol. 6, no. 4; fall, 2004.

2. Later in his article on Hammel, Kreuzer (*ibid.*) makes the case for "Crucial Trivials," phenomena once considered unimportant that can significantly influence the formation of one's self-image — a casual remark overheard in grade school, a glimpse of a domestic scene in someone else's home, a line from a campfire song, part of a scene from a movie otherwise unremembered.

3. As will be seen, Hammel followed Kreuzer's advice. This essay will conclude with a lengthy inventory of Hammel's most secret regrets, anxieties, fantasies and embarrassments.

4. Are we misreading Hammel? Grierson to the contrary, the debate about whether any form of art can provide meaningful insights into human nature is mired in subjectivity. Workman in *My Art and I* (Wholeness House, chapter 14) identifies so-called "criteria for the beneficent effects" of visual art. However, his criteria (such as "a sustainable inner peace" and "rejection of oppressive materialism") are either unverifiable, dubious and/or inadequately defined.

5. It is assumed throughout that a poem (even the present one) is a work of art regardless of its worth.

6. According to Kreuzer, Hammel's view, that love provides a ready-made identity and measure of self worth, is one of the most prevalent and damaging illusions of western civilization [chapter 1, p. 14].

7. Crocker and Wield [*The Morphing of Human Personality*, Almond House, 2001] elaborate on their position that we are all amalgams of traits that can variously recombine, sometimes unpredictably, under certain circumstances to yield sub-variants of a dominant personality. Considering the Hammel of 1977–2002 as described by Kreuzer, one is hard put to find much more than the rather bland dominant personality.

8. One consequence of the Crocker-Wield hypothesis, not yet explored in current literature and well beyond the scope of this paper, is whether there are patterns of response sufficiently recognizable, prevalent and predictable as to constitute elements of an ur-identity.[9]

9. The present writer is unclear as to the meaning of the foregoing note

10. Asked on another occasion whether he considered himself a "distinct individual" like Picasso, Maltraux replied, "I positively lack indistinction." He later elaborated, "If any one other human being, living or dead, is possessed of such qualities as to be regarded as unique or distinct, then I, by the very fact that I am not that human being, am unique and distinct." Is this consolation for Versichi's "miserable unachieving masses moving to the disposal unit on the conveyor belt of life"?

11. See Gilson and Parker, *God Made You* (Grace Press, 1996), for a detailed explanation of the Christian position that a divine creator inspires the development of individuality including the forms of human misbehaviour attributable to original sin. Adele Crossman in *All God's Children Got Warts* (Crossing Jordan Publishers, 1999) refutes multiple manifestations of original sin and rejects the role of a divine power in personality development.

12. Do you believe you are distinct and unique?

13. In the so-called Cinderella movies a woman is presented in unremarkable (and often masculine) guise until she emerges as a startling physical beauty to the astonishment of all. Is Hammel claiming he is adept at discerning such unapparent beauty in films and real life?

14. According to Kreuzer, the memories of our most traumatic experiences and the emotions associated with them, our strongest unspoken fears, our most secret aspirations, our deepest disappointments, "the dark subtexts of our lives" are the areas most in need of exploration. He favours a self-directed inventory called "cognitive sampling" to the traditional forms of therapy. (R. S. Kreuzer, *The Subtext of Your Life,* Rhye and Co., 1993)

15. The control that form exerts on emotion in a work of art is discussed at length by Appleton in her article "Emotional Distancing Through Form and Structure" (*Journal of Modern English Theatre*, spring, 1989). She especially considers the proposition that form and structure may be inhibitory from a therapeutic standpoint.

16. Appleton claims her sexuality was positively affected by several casual but unusual phenomena, an example of which was a note left her by an anonymous patron of a lounge where she worked at the age of twenty.

17. "So much heat and light is generated in the early stages of love that each party's dark side is cast in deeper darkness and is seldom suspected. But we all have a dark side. Except you and me." — Lawrence Chundra, *Romance: A Cynic's Guide* (Whine Press, 1997).

18. The full text reads: "To let a man 'have his way' is no more making love than letting plants grow is gardening. Are you listening, my dear Puffy?" (Lady Etonia Barton-North, letter to her daughter Amanda, later Amanda Billingate, Aug. 24, 1881). We are not sure why Hammel underlined this text, though Kreuzer applies it to the breakup of his marriage to Mavis.

19. Significantly, a line deleted from one of Hammel's several unpublished manuscripts reads: "It occurred to Bernice that all of life was a series of random glances made while walking rapidly past the booths in a pub."

20. Kreuzer was of the opinion, expressed in his recent public lectures, often using Hammel as an example, that our self-generated delusions about ourselves and others mar human relations more severely than knowledge of actual flaws and limitations. Nonetheless, he considered these delusions unavoidable and, in some instances, necessary for self-preservation. His colleague, Armand Kiley, called this concept "a reforestation project in which artificial trees supplant real ones" in his unpublished article "Real War in the Pseudo Woods."

21. As evidence he would apply this observation to Hammel, Merriman has written something strikingly similar elsewhere: "On the cross of love more people self-crucify than are crucified." ("Extracting the Nails," *Magma*, fall, 1995, p. 67).

22. If every reading is a misreading, as Kiley asserts, it does not follow that all misreadings are equally worthless. This one, for instance. Should the affective measure of a work of art be restricted to its impact on one's immediate conscious awareness?

23. Kiley begs the question of the relationship of art to truth. A friend of the writer was sued over an attribution in a footnote in a book. Another acquaintance had her PhD thesis disallowed because a footnote purportedly confuted a good portion of her argument. The French say truth lies in nuances. Professor Kreuzer modified that to "Truth lies in footnotes." Hellkin is notorious for having shortened Kreuzer to "Truth lies."

24. "This is as naked as I get," Hammel scribbled in one of his last diary entries. "This inventory results from the deepest excavating of which I am capable using cognitive sampling. It is compiled with great trepidation, especially the parts about my sexual proclivities, my dishonest manipulations and my self-deceptions. Thank God Mavis never had this ammo during the divorce."

25. Whether the "state of near absolute liberation" Kreuzer alleges will result and whether that condition produces sustainable benefits, remains to be seen. Though revealing his very personal inventory obviously did little for Hammel, consider developing your own such list and (a) presenting it to the person(s) you most love, (b) posting it on the internet, perhaps in a blog, or (c) making a poem of it.

HIT AND RUNS

IT COULD HAVE BEEN

He says things are "swell." She thinks
that's swell. He smokes, so she smokes.
He smokes Sportsman. She smokes Sweet
Caporal. He has no car so they walk
to movies, dances, restaurants
through the new park after supper.
They sit on the grass and smoke.
People going home late at night
see their cigarettes like fireflies
against the dark mounds of trees.

He is a hardware clerk, 28.
She is a beautician, 21.
He has those swell city moves mother
warned her about before they left
the homestead where she was born,
its roof rotting and starting to leak,
the chickens given to neighbours
for a promise of eggs. The cow
sold and slaughtered the same day.
Not a kernel of crop to fret about.

Her mother doesn't like his type.
Her sisters whisper rumours.
But she is deep down sure of him.
They've already talked of babies
and she has a list of names,
one of which is mine.

Gary Hyland

In their second summer, they wed
and now eight months later,
March frost scrawled on windows
a cold paw creeping across
the kitchen floor, the old bed's
metal frame rattles with the pulse
of my spawning and nothing else
because it's two bloody a.m.
and he is primed with liquor
and looking for a little and she's
just too rundown to resist.

And if it wasn't like that, well
given how things turned out,
it could have been. If it wasn't,
it damn well could have been.

And then they sit up and tug
sheets and blankets to their chins.
Both silent though thinking.
How come it isn't all that swell?

He lights a Sportsman. She lights
a Sweet Cap and they don't talk.

Just two dots of light in the dark
apartment, almost merging
once when they inhale together.

OR SAY

Or say they never met each other.
She marries Walter who dies young
then Del Lodge, the coal man's son.
He marries Glennis, two doors down.

The seed that would have been me
wasted in Glennis on a dry run,
the egg flushed after Walter's funeral,
my brother shut out. And my sons.

Glennis would not have wed Roland
and had Bill, Arlene and Ted.
Del would not have volunteered
and taken shrapnel at Dieppe.

Would they have done better,
raised a finer brood than ours?
Would a young man who looked
a bit like me inherit Crown Coal

in 1963, just in time
to welcome the new gas burners?
Would Glennis have twin girls
the image of my father's sister —

one who dies in a car accident
at seventeen, and the other
who runs off with a Greek pilot
and only writes at Christmas?

Gary Hyland

So many futures lost in the past.
Instead, my mother agreed to dance.
My father was delighted she did.
The rest happened as it had to.

She looked past his stained
teeth, his thinning hair. He
looked past her saucy mouth,
frowns from her mother and sisters

to the most they could make of
love for as long as they could,
and if it wasn't Hollywood, it
was still good enough for me.

GRAPE

It's not large, this grape,
the size of a marble.
It rolls along my teeth,
submitting its flesh
in supple resistance.

The vendor said this batch
of red grapes came
from Spain. I imagine
Valencia, lush fields
fading into blue hills.

There, grapes may be red.
At the fruit stall, where
they bulge
in nets like pendulous
ganglia,

they're a dusty crimson
with splotches of smoky
grey and dull green
as if the limpid outer
skins encased an olive.

Flipped by my tongue
the grape flicks off the roof
of my mouth with
a hollow smack
like a ball in a game.

Gary Hyland

Under tongue, in its
moist nest, it dreams
summer, sunlight,
the anonymity
of uncountable numbers.

From the fridge, it was
cool but now
it has the warmth
of my body. When I
choose to bite down

the soft rupture will
flood my taste buds
and I will feel my own
heat the way a tiger
eating me would taste it.

DISCUSSION LATE AT NIGHT

We make a campfire of ideas
in the cave of night.

We decide everything has a place.
All the waste, all the weeds, all the words.
Nothing dispensable, including empty space.

Death as well. To clear the way,
rejuvenate the earth
and feed the beetles.
To make an emerald of life.

Poverty? asks Ruth. Pain?
Perversion?
The eruptions of evil?
Abuse and AIDS?

Ah, the conundrums.
The corollaries of free will.
Can there be choice without error,
shots without upshots?

Until we are perfect, says Lois,
our systems will discharge such crud.

Malcolm, clever Malcolm,
suggests certain corrupt words
contaminate thoughts
and generate guck.

Gary Hyland

Malcolm, professor of a leaf on one of the twigs
of one of the branches of one of the limbs of science,
lover of precision.

Select, Malcolm, the word to ban
and someone will absolutely need it
to say something, I say.

A poet will re-invent it to fill a space.
A politician to vex the nation.
The libertarian by way of illustration.

And so long into the wine
we debate the wisdom of the world
that gave us life
and which we conclude we would not change.

Well, maybe mosquitoes.

VORTAL TOMB, POULNABRONE

1.

Brink of day and nothing green
this side of the burren in County Clare
near Galway, the sun flaring
south and east, rocks jutting
from heaves of limestone.

Later tourists will come to shoot
the tombs and utter comparisons
to the face of the moon.
                              Now it is me
and the almost sun and the tombs
filling with the thick caramel light.

O it's a haunted place they warned
some return nevermore themselves.

I give myself to that, not the fool.
The one with nothing green inside.

2.

Covert beauty in these barrens.
Gold moss robust on grey facets.
Symmetrical shadows of furrows
down rock faces. Limestone histories.
Chalky excrescence on the shady
sides of stones. The sky bronze
and orange and umber. Huge
slabs of the dolman in silhouette.

The absence of excess. Marvels
of the dim and the dull. Arid profusion.

I have no guide, no text to explain
the glaciation, the Karst drainage
system. I decipher memories
of absences and pungent emptiness.

3.

    From stone we grind our lives.
    Four thousand Christless years
 of hunting and rituals and burials
 and fifteen hundred more beneath
the priestly ways of Rome mean nothing
        on these gaping wastes.
  Lichen pale grey. Runnels on rock.

  Who was he, hero of the raths,
  whose axe made meat of flesh
     and splintered bone?

     Who was she
 he met behind the great heaved
 stones? Wraiths on this wind.

       Whispering.

4.

Windalong voices.
                        Place of death.

Gust smitten.
                        Words of wrath.

Air in a rush.
                        Cursed of Da.

Ears in a thrash.
                        Da's red eyes.

Nothing bends.
                        Ashes of rage.

When we set our slings aside
these stones will fly.
When we stop our killing
death will die.

5.

The wind rattles my jacket.
It slaps my chest and arms. That lone
noise like a flag's call to combat.
Fright in the blood. A short hike from the slow
green silence beneath the sea.

East of here a farmer's tractor split
the capstone of a buried cist
and opened to the sky a grave
filled three thousand years before.

With a rush the spirit swooped
out and gusts across this land
forever seeking haven. As we, soon
to follow, search each day. This memory
wind-implanted while the sun fumes.

6.

A place can own you.
Alone with the nameless dead
I drift out of today
towards their graves
yet away from fear.

Surrendering
I feel unbound.
Freedom is a union, not
unfettering. It is another way
the earth can have you.
Sublime submission.

It is the way of making things.
Stepping outside to be within again.
What unbinds ensnares.

7.

Six miles from the closest cottage,
I turn my back to the rocks
and there are more. But I gain
an angle on the wind. Its attack
flattens jacket and slacks
against my body. On the other
side they bulge and flap.

A land grey-brown and bleak,
rain-leached, vast — the burren.
Another country's wasteland
familiar as my nightly dream.
I've been here many times —
the desolate stretches, the wind's
lonesome blast. Home.

Gary Hyland

8.

A taffy sky with three white swans
winging to the sea. No place for hangings,
drownings, burials. They found ways,
to kill, ways to dump the dead.

When the seasons allow, in fissures
filled with meagre soil, grow rare
mountain avens, orchids, maidenhair.

Near what I think is the path back
a sink hole and on its edge a fringe
of grass so sparse it has no shadow.

You will take the haunted burren
with you, the image-laden wind,
the wailings of gods forsaken.
And they will take you to your end.

RAVEL IN AUTOMOBILE ACCIDENT
   — *1932 headline*

Five years later, he is lost, unable
to hear more than a baffled cello
when others move their mouths.
And is he, too, muffled below
their range of hearing? He can no
longer tell — his, theirs, the music
they say he wrote, the music of past
masters tumble in a panic.

Before the mangle, music came
in streams of light congealing.
Now, nothing. Instruments tuned
by maniacs to squealing.
What is it to be alive, a myth,
with your life lost? All zero
if your dreamless nights cannot
cobble another *Boléro?*

Surgeons, slice into the dark,
searching for notes too long
astray to make ashen strains spark
again. They find no path to song.
They cannot locate the nodes of
composition and mend the cause
of his loss. He dies with the love
of music the last of his flaws.

Gary Hyland

MILDLY MANIC:
A POET MEETS JOHN NASH IN McLEAN HOSPITAL,
BOSTON, 1959

1.

No confession, a depiction of a common condition,
to say I was not myself when I met Nash.
Is anyone ever fully himself and if so when?
Nor was he himself, tormented half the time,
muttering into his shoulder. We've misplaced ourselves
in this loony bin for the nation's Brahmin
where one is inspected, injected, restrained, debrained,
edified, medified, mental blocked and electroshocked.
I said that.
          He said you think rhyme makes sense.
It's merely a false algorithm. I don't recall my response.
I think I slandered numbers. A long silence
after that. It was in one of the corridors
that our symptoms first mingled like vapours.

P.S. When recovering, from time to time,
unpredictably, I relapse into rhyme.

Hands Reaching in Water

2.

I suspect our duck-billed psychiatrists
conspired a non-paranoidal plot to couple us so
we'd each cancel the other's derangement,
balance at last the two irrational equations.

Our uncommon encounter was in the common room,
me in flagrant jabber, Nash nodding and peering
at my slippers, not listening, not talking at first.
Becalmed with Thorazine, or so I thought.

He reeked of smoke that evoked my uncle's parlour,
men propped with pipes and cigars explaining
what was wrong with my father.

I had to tell him I had lied about the juicing,
as we call the electroshock treatments.
Since Stanton took over a few years back
all that voodoo had been vanquished.
I gave him my spiel about faking
one's way through psychotherapy
and the rights of those forcibly committed.
Oh, that perked him up considerably.

3.
               The door, the baseboards,
the window frames are painted spring-tree green
to soothe agitated brains. The paint has splintered
and the shreds collect in the unswept corners
like leaves waiting to become metaphors.

I think that it should be recorded for history
though it didn't seem historic. History seldom does.
Quaint the way Eisenhower thinks the future
will read his golf scores. Such a hole-in-one.
When I get snide like that I know I'm on the mend.
Maybe Nash perked me after all. I remember now:
I suggested that he not fire integers at a rhymester
with *trash, hash, crash, bash* and *smash* in the wings.

Flaunting his math biceps, he tried to demonstrate
the "simultaneity of the universe," muttered about
"an infinite regress," scribbled hieroglyphics,
more symbols than numbers, parentheses galore.
When done, he claimed he'd elaborated (and improved)
someone's proof that time does not exist. I couldn't resist
asking why the watch on his wrist. His answer was
something about the linear bias of the brain.

Should we care if time is a figment or myth? We are born.
We die. Things happen in between. If there is no sequence
of moments to divide events, as Nash asserts, what does?
If time's a mirage, we still damn ourselves to its confines.
If there is no early or late, how did I miss supper last night?
Without before and after how to measure my recovery?

I think he's haunted by echoes of zeros.

Hands Reaching in Water

4.

He fell into another silence when I observed that while
I understood none of his scratching, his words indicated
that he was confusing the non-transitive verb to be
with the mathematical symbol for equals and that
to say Nash is tedious, is not to say Nash is tedium.
In other words, he finally said, you reject this proof
on the same basis as contemporary metaphysicians
reject the ontological proof of God's existence,
because it makes being a verb rather than a pure
copula attributing a quality and not a category.
I allowed as God could be a verb, a noun, a dishrag
for all I knew, that ontology is as ontology does,
and metaphysics begets inanity/insanity,
not to mention indolence, intolerance, and indigestion.

I suspect he's a genius in his own tree but germane
retorts are not his forté. He called me a hack
and dove into a calculating silence.

5.

Dancing over time we smash into God.
It starts when he says that God occupies
reality only in the mind of man. Ah ha,
I say, and does the mind not partake of the real
and therefore by virtue of the principle of containment
is God not real? He chuckles. *Thank you. You have
just endorsed the so-called illusory creatures
whose presumed nonexistence landed me here.*

At last a retort worthy of his pretensions.
He may be loony but his mind ain't porridge.
We get to discussing how one tells the real
from the unreal. Nash's gestures become livelier.
I have always thought it foolish to try proving
God's existence by using the brain, so like
the chair trying to deduce the carpenter.
The brain itself is the best evidence —
its complexity, its alacrity, its capacity.
I love my brain even when she stomps my heart.

6.

Nash is puzzled by poetry except as a game.
I quote Lycidas, Lord Weary, extemporize.
Verse is corpuscular in me. One thinks of *curse*
or *adverse*, some flimsy spider wit on which
to rig the water-skin illusion of control.
The grand affliction of writers,
their blank pages being divine slates
for meticulous mistakes,
poets the worst, their mirage that they
have ordered every syllable for the best.

They age into righteous certitude
like Nash's hierarchy of mathematicians.
Three or more comprise a school or,
when at Yale or Harvard, a pantheon,
their babbling proclaimed on minion wings,
their technologies infallible.

The omniscient point-of-view seeps backward
from our pens into our veins
deluding us into thinking we understand
the nuances of brains like Nash's,
and though to the manor born, I detest this gall.
The all-knowing garble. The anemic omnipotence.

I renounce control. The tidy genetic stanza.
The poet who deliberately plans a
long rhyming extravaganza
makes me want to vomit. (He bans a
temptation to use *bonanza*.)

Oh, I'm a bowl of healing confections
rife with bilious infections.

Gary Hyland

7.

When I'm mildly manic, as this week, I squeeze
my hands between my knees and exercise
restraint sufficient to convince the shrinksters
I'm in recovery mode.
                         I write letters, verse, notes
to strangers, stairways, trees and post them
in the latrine.

Manic, I can work magic. Translate a book a day,
over night jot an entire play.
                         Manics generate
the most progress in the least time with the highest
collateral grief. We are the agitated hearts of the world
beating triple time.
                         O rip us up. O rip us out.

Love wilts while we chicken-trot obsessions.

We charm or agitate the sane, amaze bystanders.

Last night a memo to Nash:
You are not crazy, John. Your brain has children
illegitimately and you legitimize them
with attention. Ignore them and Herr
Brain Doctors will do the same for you.
                         I don't
expect he can. He will be here when I return.

Hands Reaching in Water

In sessions I am semi-calm, but not
serene, not the pill-graded blotto mind.

I could untether and explode all over McLean,
but I want a discharge.
                              Time to walk in time again
with a sweet tremor where once a tempest
vexed the workings in the old clock tower.

HIT AND RUNS

1.

He waves to the man waving at him.
The man drives his car where he cannot go.
He knows he cannot go as he waves.
The man has his clothes, his wallet,
a letter he wrote in his pocket.

He waves to the man and wants to go.
The man in his vehicle will travel far
and never return. The address
on the letter is where he wants to go.

His waving says, "Goodbye, dear fool."
The man waves: "I'm more honest than you."
The letter has no return address.

He wants to go while staying.
He wants to return without leaving.

He waves to the man in his car.

2.

Someone else drives his car.
He relaxes with the driver at the wheel
even though his old motor might die.
He hums and skims his mail
and tries to look rich reading his bills.

In the back he reads what he must pay.
A lurch and a thump.
The driver accelerates.
"We've hit someone," he says.

"He walked onto the road waving."
He glances back at his shocked face.
He wants to jump out, to return and help.

"He wasn't watching his step,"
he says as they lunge into the dark.

He tries to look like someone else.

Gary Hyland

3.

The body crumpled on the wet pavement
is his. He stands there looking
at the body crumpled, hardly bleeding,
at himself — fetal, eyes closed,
a heap of waste against the curb.

He does not know which is his body.
He wants them both, the one at peace
and the one in which blood
still surges, the blood of desire.

To be in desire. To be past desire.
He wants them both. To feel the thrum.
To rest undamaged, beyond alarm.

Crumpled against the curb and beside
they wait for him to decide.

He stands there looking.

4.

He gazes to where she might have been
and points the car into darkness and rain,
getting away fast with the passenger
in the back seat beginning to hum a strain
neither of them can fill with words.

It beguiles him, the tune without words
that the passenger sounding so familiar
hums, his eyes looking familiar
in the rearview mirror as they speed

towards a woman pale and startled
on the road. He veers past her
by steering up the wrong street

into traffic he swerves to avoid.
As they careen into air

the passenger is not in the mirror.

Gary Hyland

5.

The car flipped, him dangling, strapped inside.
Ribs surprised, jagged and white.
Too much speed, rain, the traffic.
The ceiling soaked with blood.
An arm that hangs without feeling.

Everything reversed, fibrous with pain.
A judge will say he went too fast.
Strapped inside and running away.
The song. Those sleep-stealing
eyes. The mirror filling too fast

with the backseat face
he watched at the wrong time.
The body? The woman?

Someone mutters his name.
He forces himself to look out,

sees wild, gaping eyes. His.

6.

Riddled and lame, he will not drive again,
toes and cane tapping the edges of things.
He had been running away the wrong way.
Accidents by volition?
The passenger must have died.

He had been dreaming the purest dream —
breezeless sunlit love, no one who limps,
humming the tune too wonderful
for words, the passenger's song.

The passenger in the mirror also
humming. Growing luminous
the tune leaked into light.

The passenger rests deep
in the earthen night,

humming the tune he loves.

Gary Hyland

MOTIVES FOR BEAUTY

MOTIVES FOR BEAUTY

1.

The tiger is beautiful
in order to kill —

a liquefaction
of sun in the jungle

sinuous with shadows,
sensuous in vines.

In the half-light of leaves
he is what you do not

see before being slammed
down, the pain that ends

pain. Your flesh, your blood,
the price of beauty.

Your brain, silvery gel
inside its cracked shell,

the artist, the priest.
Without your sacrifice

beauty would starve
eating shadows on a limb.

Gary Hyland

2.

The violet is beautiful
so insects will pander

to its lust. Shape
colour, texture, combine

in the beauty we admire,
traits of curve and line.

We fabricate so we
can muster praise,

pleasure, ease, honour,
plunder, power.

First delight is pure,
an interval of joy

before a claim is made,
before a flash of light

lunges from midnight
onto the hunter.

DREAM PLACE

He lies in long grass, ferns, vetch
that have never been ploughed or grazed,

stays all day, breathes sage and later
gazes at the low moon's illusions.

A hawk spirals, black on sun-blazed wings.
A gopher snake tongues air, threads away.

He looks at the sky until he can look
no longer — slow cumulus billows floating

in a cavernous brilliance.
Under his arm other colours burst —

orange, green, white, silver-gray —
of primrose, phlox, moss and lichen

blending as if spun in a clenched eye,
the abundance, the teeming intensity.

Two grouse huff by, a skunk detours
to a pile of rocks, crows reconnoitre.

Wind strums his hair while ants, beetles,
spiders, provide a perspective

in which he is the mountain range.
Coyotes skitter at the border of his scent.

On a further verge, a gentle rumble —
the distant percussion of hooves.

Gary Hyland

CRIME SITES

Murders of poverty and of privilege
happen here with equal frequency.
They found the body of an abused waif
among that gnarl of saskatoon bushes
where the river spills silt every spring.
The next fall in that place beyond the reeds
the remains of a rancher's impulsive wife.
Bloodlines back to Cheapside and Crown Hill.
In your haste to leave, you will cross over
other sites.
               Archaeologists say the world
is choked with crime scenes. All we need is a cause
and a stone. The river, full of predators,
flows on. In town the doctor's house burns
with secrets the ashes will later disclose.

LAST QUARTER MAN

The shingles on his roof he swore
    were immune to moonlight.
Rainfall made them gleam
    a dark sheen in the dark night.

The porch sagged in the middle
    like an unhappy brow.
Rain flowed there and streamed
    down on the drooping steps

soaking no one. No one came.
    Weeds leaned onto the porch
as if to sip. In snowtime,
    one set of footsteps to and fro.

So dense so close were the trees
    that looking from his window
summer or winter his was
    the only image to be seen.

Music stayed out in the woods
    and ravines, wild grass blades
humming, and harmonies
    of finches, bees and leaves.

Inside, absence of moon and sun.
    Footsteps in rooms. The air
thin with things unspoken
    by the slim last quarter man.

Gary Hyland

WOMAN AFTER WOMAN

Those days, when a woman squinted any direction
across a field or down a two-rut trail
she could see for twenty miles,

and when she did (pick your compass point)
there would be another woman in a doorway
looking the same direction

for someone overdue, for new neighbors
arriving by rail, for salvation from
the weather or day after day sameness,

and past that other woman, another
and so on, woman after woman looking
down the line in a relay of hope.

GUYS FROM HERE

1. *Lionel*

By seventeen he'd worn his own rut in Main Street
and the cops knew where to find him any time of day.
Worked a year at the service station
changing oil for his former teachers, the parents of friends,
before hitchhiking to the coast.

There, in time, he made it big,
at least enough for him. Secretaries,
gardeners, housekeepers, accountants.

He could recite five reasons
he'd never not on your life not once ever
return. And he didn't.
It would, after all, be going backward downhill.

As we walk down the steps from the deck
with the twelve-person hot tub to the barbecue deck.
I say to my wife, "A bit of Napoleon there."
She adds, "And pity Josephine."

Gary Hyland

2. *Herman*

At a certain point his life turned
ninety degrees and he did not resist.
He followed his friends from a prairie town
that no longer exists to the metropolis
where he married glamour. Two children,
drugs and alcohol followed before the divorce.
He remarried sensibly and settled down.
Then his daughter overdosed and died.
Moving into himself he saved himself.
He lives alone now in a Vancouver apartment
inside a nonexistent town.

3. *Travis*

He has me outpowered.
His decisions can make me suffer.
My decisions don't excite his system.
He has 162 employees with computers or guns.
His wife has had two facelifts.
He outwits cancer smoking small black cigars
half-way down.
His silver Lexus has a back seat refreshment panel.
He's had open heart surgery
in Houston.
He believes he has me figured out:
I am a supplicant who envies him.
I am but I don't.
I have my own perks and peculiarities,
my own maladies.
I was never after power.
Though I wouldn't mind the Lexus.

4. *Eugene, Delmer, the Other Older Ones*

White-topped with pink scalps
or bald, quivery on new hips and knees,
skin splotched and creased,
they clomp
into the garden party
on chrome appliances
that gleam like weapons.

Get them a chauffeured limousine.
Get them curvaceous companions.
Reverse the rearview mirror.
Toss the implements, supplements and medications.
Fill hampers with food, drink and diapers.
Drive them west one last time,
the sun blazing off the bumper
like something remembered at last.

THE ILLUSION OF GOING FORWARD

As we drive the prairie west
the city arrives in stages.
A luster in the distant sky,
then beacons from buildings,
a necklace spangled on a ledge,
becoming distinct beads of light.
Beyond, a dark expanse of future.

The earth bends from our eyes
rising and falling away
like a shy notion.

The land turns into time
and returns us to earth
with its illusions — an erased
horizon, great ranges
of wind-shaped clouds,
hills massing into legends.

The earth will do this, give us
myths about itself.
Others we fashion
in imitation, believe so firmly
we live depleted lives
with wind-squinted eyes
beguiling us that we are on the level.

Gary Hyland

STAR OF [insert name of a once-popular TV show] DIES

He did this or that, the star, and then he died.
So the stories run, smug digests of his life —

public man for a public that craves the pain
that twisted him; disdain tempered applause.

The heart of fame contorted by celebrity
spills its contents onto the floodlit stage.

No life without a price commensurate.
No benefits grow, no curse slices, no charm exalts

without a blade that cuts away some flesh.
Not being known is the toll of being known

and those who hail, mock or ape them thrive
with their addictions, divorces and disease.

We know of this and still we lift them up.
They kill to reach the coliseum.

§

They kill to reach the coliseum.
We know of this and still we lift them up

with their addictions, divorces and disease,
and those who hail, mock or ape them thrive.

Not being known is the toll of being known.
Without a blade that cuts away some flesh

no benefits grow, no curse slices, no charm exalts.
No life, without a price commensurate,

spills its contents onto the floodlit stage,
the heart of fame contorted by celebrity

that twisted him. Disdain tempered applause.
Public man for a public that craves the pain —

so the stories run, smug digests of his life —
he did this or that, the star, and then he died.

ALTERNATE CANCER THERAPY

She says the metal bowl from ancient
Egypt encircled with pre-Ptolemaic
symbols, when struck with a padded mallet,
shivers through every cell of her body.
To which her husband raises an eyebrow:
More of the holistic therapy drivel
that he's finding so hard to tolerate.
As if vibrations from some pharaoh's
salad bowl could shunt death aside.
He says he places faith only in hard-core
science, forgetting, it seems, that research
shows our body mass is mostly water,
and that as a boy he would sit by the shore
rapt by sounds channeled on the lake.

STARTING LINES

He was invited to start the race
a pistol shot into the clouds
the runners' calves taut with speed

There was a time he ran the races
trained on frozen roads
and in rain with fine-pointed cleats
that left perfect impressions
He outran the pain
and won and was acclaimed
and coached the young
how to make themselves
a blur in the sun

A one-armed man functions well enough
aiming a gun at the sky
less difficult than saluting or praying
or running unbalanced
slicing half the air away

He bogged with time
slowness staked its claim
inclines steepened and impeded
No one listens when no one knows
the seasons he bettered the pack
all those pennants in the breeze over his head

The pistol is an honour bestowed
because someone told someone to be kind
all well enough and good
He brushes dust from the collar

Gary Hyland

and crest of the old blazer
He dons once more the club tie
exchanges genuine for imitation
loads more than noisy ammunition
And there beside the starting blocks
with men in caps craning and ladies in bonnets
officials behind binoculars in booths
the numbered lads trembling like lovers
to be first into the future
strangers all
There where once the cup was his
he puts the muzzle of the alternate mechanism
an inch in front of his ear
and pulls the trigger
and one more time
is first across the line

That is what he fancies
in a flash between orders at the pub

What he will do when the time arrives
is up in the air

SHOCK

She says she loved him so much
she kicked him several good ones
in the ribs, spine, and stomach
as he lay there dead
on their living room floor
having departed without so much
as a doctor's note,
a prescription,
no sign of illness.

Terror will do that —
hold you up
turn you against grief, against
love in a fury of tears.
The world buggered again.

She said she screamed at him
called him a coward
for sneaking off with the valuables.
In fact, she said, if god had been there
there might have been another stomping.

Gary Hyland

REACH

All her life she cherished beauty which meant
late arrivals, lost fortunes, and privation.
And was herself a beauty men stopped for.
The songs she sang circled their distances.
Her shrines: the wild pronghorns west and south,
their flashes of white rump; the off-road coulee
where she strolled through hawthorn, birch and poplar;
the willowed lakeshore of mallards and herons;
sky-cracking summer storms; winter white-outs;
roadside stops to gather primrose, larkspur,
buck-bean, yarrow, harebell, violets.
Now long-throated orchids, mauve and white,
on her casket, her daughters and their daughters
beguiled in the compass of her music.

STAKES IN THE RIVER

A BRIEF HISTORY OF ZERO

1.

Before zero, holes in skulls,
mouths of caves did not
add up. There were spaces
we could not scale, murders
more than we could number.

Like eggs in the sands of India,
zeros waited to emerge —
disciplined citizens
in strict formations
for market calculations.

2.

From Babylon the Greeks
wrested a caravan of mere
plunder. The real wealth was
zero rattling like a golden egg
in one playful brain.

Its flawless arms held nothing
perfectly. It surged beyond one,
crushed old scores and ledgers
and sculpted infinity —
the orbits of planets and stars.

3.

Mad prophets saw it at the bottom
of sacred wells. Bid disciples
cast off sinful earth, destroy
their herds, kill enemies
and themselves in joy.

Zero where a village thrived,
and where the crops had waved.
Zero where the huts were razed,
zero in the cradles
and in survivors' eyes.

Adding zeros Hitler foresaw
the precise future of the Jews,
a solution in tall and tidy rows.
His skull still dreams blue-eyed
boys goose-stepping under halos.

Gary Hyland

4.

Zero on/zero off yields
complex computer codes,
remote nuclear devices, digital
intimacies, the age of space,
and voice-activated toilets.

Zero's what the earth will total
in not so many zeros aligned
behind an unrelenting one —
a perfectly oxidized disc
rapidly spinning nowhere.

Hands Reaching in Water

INFINITY'S TWIN

Zero isn't nothing. Portal to
infinity. Cut throat. Fatal code. Noose.

Churchmen, placing halos over the heads
of saints, sent crusaders against Satan's

cipher, this whirlpool mouth of the void
sure to devour all heaven and hell.

Zero's the black hole that swallows black holes
and astronomers. It ambushes cultures.

Minus 273.16
degrees, absolute zero, kills the concept

of freezing the subatomic boogey,
once the ardent dream of physicists.

On this thin round line depends our belief
in deep space, the big bang, infinity, God.

Gary Hyland

MIAMI HOLIDAY

Behind hotels flavoured peach and orange and lime
the breezeless shore features only two pelicans
feeding in the shallows by the pier and a few
inclined umbrellas barely concealing lovers.
The evening air is wetter than any the boy has breathed.
At last, he spies a phone booth for calling home
and telling the folks he's arrived okay. He wants to joke
about the snow up there which is what he is doing
when the pistol barrel is jammed against his throat.
Mom asking, "What did you say, dear? I didn't hear,"
while the boy with the pistol snarls, "Money. All of it."
He says, "Just a minute," annoying the pistol boy who
needs to please his mocking pals and score some crack
real quick, so he pulls the trigger. They split
back to the boulevard leaving the receiver dangling
over the sand where the dead boy lies bleeding.
Above him, a voice is repeating his name
over and over, the question mark becoming a screech,
which the closest pelican acknowledges,
turning, fish in beak, and blinking at the beach.

VISION: FOOT DESCENDING
— *Sept. 11, 2001*

Darkness gleams like oiled calfskin
beneath the descending foot.
Thieves shake, promise to return their loot.

Midnight drenches everything.

Full of absence the sky rains ashes.
Smiling innocents shower in blood.
Hope surges through them like embalming fluid.

A priest lifts his arms, simulates a tree.
He would be an angel out to show the way —
the nations waving, a forest of salvation.

Someone unearths a sacred song
that grows roots and puts eagles back in the sky,
but the words fade in the air.

Some believe sleep is a tunnel to sunlight.

The stars shoot into each other
and pinwheel into the corners of night
like sparks when a fire is stomped.

It's the terrible beauty screams an old man.
He trembles beneath a faucet
spraying blood. *At last,* he shouts. *At last.*

The blood gleams, tastes like wine.
It never stains.
Those who bathe in it thin into oblivion.

Others writhe, trying to dance on bleeding stumps.

Sleep, now, sleep the dreamed-for sleep.
There is no need to close your eyes.

INTERVIEWEES, SEPT. 11, 2001

A movie. A nightmare. Surreal.
Those cornered on the street
grope for words that fit.
Surreal. A movie. Repeat.

Clobbered into cliché
they shuffle to the mike:
nightmare, surreal, a movie —
all victims sound alike.

Pupils scoped to a dot
trying their best to rally
with tortured images caught
from Poe, Wells, and Dali.

Gary Hyland

HUDSON RIVER BREEZES
  — *Sept. 14, 2001*

The breezes noticed first and told the birds.
For days updrafts spilt them left and right.
After they had dispersed the soot and dust
people marveled how morning
                              filled West Street,
its pavement and doorways ashen in the sun,
and spilled out onto the river, looking
uncertain without its matching stripes.
                              Breezes
piped the moaning of a woman in Battery Park,
her voice wavering but holding like a flag.

Now their on-shore nudging teases Broadway
and ruffles Fulton Market unimpeded.
                              But
still, something is there. Now the shadow
of a great noise hangs in the air, as if an echo
of concrete and steel were welded to the sky.

WE KILL WELL

How the cold breath of a gun barrel
turns pungent after it has discharged
and made a spray of bone and brain.

Where are we killing today, men?
Kabul, Rwanda, Chiapas, Darfur?
Whose turn today?

   Protestants, Muslims, Catholics,
   peasants, pickpockets, poets,
   leftists, centrists, rightists,
   the student passing by
   the man who said *Enough*
   the woman who said *Why*
   their orphaned infant
   the journalist
   blacks, whites, pintos, palominos,
   instigators, agitators, escalators.

No sailing today, lads.
River's full of swollen bodies.

No malaria shots today, chaps.
Some of the guys shot up the nurses.

No beer today.
The irregulars bombed the regulars at Sid's.

Gary Hyland

Not one glass unbroken.
Not a spattered chair left upright.

Who shelled the boys who scrub the streets
and who will scour their blood?

No bathing today, my sweet.
The well with rotting children reeks.

BORDEN AND MORRIS IN 2104

> *But it was daylight.*
> *In the boughs of trees*
> *space hung about like washing.*
> *Through the snow*
> *faces went by like flags before a fear.*
> — P. K. Page
> "Failure at Tea"

The veranda where they sat
wore a membrane of factory soot.
Someone making something yet.
Misshapen owls began to hoot.
But it was daylight

smeared with ash and dust
enough to smudge the sun
and stain the dwarfed and twisted buds
that drooped but clung
in the boughs of trees.

"Is that snow or smog?" Morris said.
"Same thing," replied Borden.
The syllables dropped and spread
as if oracular, words in
space hung about like washing.

Gary Hyland

on a line. And soon a grey downfall
was slanting in a fretful breeze.
They could hear the compost ravens call
like waves of wounded infantries

through the snow.
Still people worried up the broken streets
and wild dogs foraged on the strand.
While Borden and Morris lapsed to sleep
sirens arced into the night and
faces went by like flags before a fear.

STAKES IN THE RIVER
A day of rotations, after James Richardson

       1.
Time stolen is the best time.

       2.
Holding on to afternoons is the hardest holding.

       3.
Staying home, the most demanding journey.

       4.
Time begrudged, the saddest time.

       5.
Time accelerates travel.

       6.
Despair says I cannot do it all. Joy says I cannot do it all.

       7.
Love and time are one.

       8.
Distance becomes time; nibbles love.

       9.
For a time you sat on God's lap. When was that?

       10.
Genius is giving others the kind of time they need.

       11.
I cannot touch you without touching time.

       12.
You confess to squandering time to validate your potential.

13.
A still night — stones fall from the wall of memory.

14.
Drudgery degrades time.

15.
A wound that does not heal over time is not a wound — it is you.

16.
How fast from *adore* to *abhor*?

17.
Time heals as snow heals — one colour that blurs and blunts.

18.
They give most who give time.

19.
The writer craves your time. You crave. . . ?

20.
Try not to hear what is not said before it is not said.

21.
Seeking to comprehend time is time lost.

22.
Art undoes time. A stake in the river.

23.
The last interruption forestalls all others.

24.
In the end, enough time has elapsed since the start.

BY THE FIFTEENTH COSMOLOGICAL DECADE

> The universe will pass through a series of eras before the end of life as we know it, two astrophysicists said Wednesday.
> — Canadian Press, Jan. 16, 1997

Pale stars rotate their rubble:
cold debris, bone dust, stone dust,
matter moving matter that was us.

Then one by one they wink out,
break formation into space
for ten times as much time as ever was.

Black holes the size of galaxies flee
each other flinging microscopic
particles in a sea of radiation.

When your lover treats you
like a regrettable habit,
when the boss picks yet another
nit from the days you swap
for weekends, and your body
incubates
untreatable lethal ailments,
remember this:

Gary Hyland

by the 15th cosmological decade
not a particle of anything left
will resemble your boss or contain
in its most subatomic recesses
a wisp of your existence

or

a super consciousness complete
with infinite serenity
will harbour a blip of energy
that your brain perfected
from this heap of sludge

either way
those things that wrench your guts
today by that tomorrow
you should judge

of course you may still fret about
your kids, your credit rating,
your puppy's parvovirus shots

but

if Cuddles dies in furry agony
and your kids become post-nasal drips
and your dreams dwindle to dung,
it can be comforting to know
that by the 15th cosmological decade
none of it will mean a whiff of shit.

HANDS REACHING IN WATER

HEROES IN COFFINS

Down fell the bold ones, too many, too often
Till not one was left and no one to implore.
There'll be no more kissing of heroes in coffins.

Imbued with belief, blind to all caution,
Advancing a cause in their fictions of war,
Down fell the bold ones, too many, too often.

Take down the pictures of flags held aloft in
A struggle the orphans refuse to explore.
There'll be no more kissing of heroes in coffins.

Most of them nameless, a few not forgotten,
those some admired and chose to adore.
Down fell the bold ones, too many, too often.

Open the portals, let clean breezes waft in.
Their lethal impatience no longer ignore.
There'll be no more kissing of heroes in coffins.

Causes turn cancerous, integrity softens.
Righteousness burned, no flame can restore.
Down fell the bold ones, too many, too often.
There'll be no more kissing of heroes in coffins.

Gary Hyland

THE FRAGILE THINGS

Our dreams subside to compromise.
Damn the faltering fallibility
that condemns the fragile things we prize.

Justice comes plunging from flak-pocked skies
and freedom is conscripted for democracy.
Our dreams subside to compromise.

Who's left to challenge the disarming lies
spun by the contrary faculty
that condemns the fragile things we prize?

While wars swat innocents like flies
on our slopes of self-made misery
our dreams subside to compromise.

The illusion we are masters defies
our chronic attempts at mastery.
That condemns the fragile things we prize.

We flower lush intentions to disguise
the transgressions we are loathe to see.
Our dreams subside to compromise
that condemns the fragile things we prize.

HANDS REACHING IN WATER
or
THE SHORT RULE OF THE PHILOSOPHER-KINGS

1.
In time form is all we have — the alphabet, a clock, our bodies.

2.
On their way to other forms. Excising excess.

3.
Annihilation by gradation.

4.
A splotch of water drying outside in.

5.
Spaces between realities dilating.

6.
Silence inflating.

7.
Our children angry at the absence of meaning: that means nothing.

8.
They think they know what they think they know.

9.
Never one thing. Absolutely.

10.
Hands reaching in water, bubbles of sound break, evaporate.

Gary Hyland

11.
Action and sadness are not options. Their shapes too vague.

12.
The clockwork of poverty makes everyone poor.

13.
Solace: surplus poverty will not increase your poverty.

14.
Flaws of concentration and distribution create scarcity.

15.
One thinks of rain. The absence of rain.

16.
A flood is surplus only because of where it happens.

17.
Too much rain to relocate, the containers too small.

18.
The sun voracious for virtue.

19.
Want is the presence of absence.

20.
The principles of economics, the tenets of justice, are natural forms.

21.
Let us convene and dispense acceptable replicas of natural justice.

22.
Let us parse definitions to vapours creating a glut of frustration.

23.
Too many distinctions baffle precision.

24.
Language ex-communicates.

25.
An ancient Latin phrase explains that injustice partakes of eternity.

26.
A clock conscious of these things could never keep time.

ARGUMENTS IN THE GARDEN OF PRAYER

1.

So many frogs are extravagant with song
the sky is crammed. A calculation might
reveal at any given moment at least
twelve to be in natural harmony.

The Meadowlark on the barbed wire
sings so I will look away from her nest
out to where the grass reaches my knees.

Here it is trimmed, exposing badger holes
snugged to the concrete cap across a grave.

Maybe twenty tombstones. Half of them my kin.

They carried her name before my mother,
unknown to her, those in this other place.

Easy to believe lives of peace and ease.
Beyond, in disagreement, wheat sags in the heat.

2.

The equation of prayer is to seed and reap.
Mulch with hosannas and orthodox mantras,
weed out distractions and focus attention
on the divine presence, which may not be
corporeal in a five-star heaven.

Ablution removes impurities
that inhibit the yield. Kneel when you plant
your petitions, kneel to weed and to receive
blessings, kneel with care in the thorny
blackberries that resemble small grenades.

This compact dogwood bursting like a torch
from the snow presents a grace in winter
we might otherwise not savour, had we not
sown it in faith two short summers ago.

3.

A crisis late at night. Someone dying.
The end of something you love. It is always
cold. You are alone and sometimes crying,
the indifferent world in its slumber bliss.
Confined to a cage in the tower, your mind
rattles and clangs against the metal bars
while your eyes, white to the world, look on.
Rats scutter inside your guts, eating, shitting.
God wants to bring you peace, a soothing song
but you are as jagged as a broken knife.
You would stroke your own hand in comfort
if the crusty sores did not erupt.
Dawn will dawn. People will awake and kiss.
One might kiss you. If only you had lips.

4.

His death is all you know. Meanwhile the garden
flavours the morning gold, green, indigo,
as you sit in a daze and cannot name
the plants sown when he was still in bloom.
You slept and while you dreamed of him he died.
Colour, taste, touch are mute and all the words
fall into winter, white and cold. Your prayers
freeze on the line, flimsy incantations.
They need tomorrow, soil, water, the sun,
all of which have gone to imitations.
Those ants that scurry across the stones
have a destination, will make sense
of each perception, but you cannot speak
words like *mother, son* and *resurrection*.

5.

This morning's nittering songbirds I commend
to cats. My legs are pale and numb with death.
I have pissed in all my pools. I will kill myself.
No one cares. I don't care. The earth just wants
another mouthful.
                      Your so-called gifts are killing
me too slowly. Sunshine is a blast of hell.
You don't believe me. Think you know more.
I puke on your hypothetical Plan.

Okay. Okay. You win again. I recant,
rub my shins and knees to shivering.

Behold the glory of my creation —
my heart's a swamp, birds and bugs plunge in stench,
reeking shreds of flesh droop from my ass,
blisters purl my cheeks, eruptions of love.

6.

Honour the land, honour God. Who is God
of this fire-blackened hollow? Not even
the ants have returned. A dried thistle rattles
by a black rock. That is all but for ash
on the wind. No bush. No trees. Burnt grass
bristle stiff and dusting underfoot.
A dismal scoop of hell. The place where Satan
laughed and scorched belief to the roots.
In the black midst, death on death, the skeleton
of a fox, white, delicate as scripture.
A language untranslatable now.
You know the code will be broken, meaning
teased into greenness. But today
you must walk away. You must leave it behind.

7.

Thick heat rides the high noon wind
that slams my face. My camel has six
cylinders and twenty-four loan payments.
I start the air conditioning. That's progress.

Because I'm not sweating on a gangly,
cud-spitting, farting beast and foraging
for rats, you exist. I am going forward
with Merton and Chardin in the back seat.

You ride with us because I need to believe
we are moving beyond camels and cars
and holy massacres to some transcendence.

In a blink the universe expanded
from a marble to every single thing.
That's when we think we heard your fingers snap.

8.

That was not you I glimpsed. The mind complexes
itself, a song that spins the same phrase
past intricacy into dullness.
                              Is that
your trouble or triumph? This thing that thinks
it sees you? Or is you?
                          The accidents
we name and align into systems in our
puny shots at heaven?
                        Only in sleep
am I certain of you. All night you spoke
and I was not comforted. Woke too soon, sore,
confused, the room dim, thinking you might be
a committee, a wired neuronal web
making wiser, more generous choices.
Hence the trinity of specialists theory.

Presumptuous? I wouldn't think of it.

9.

Of course, you have to love yourself. What else
is worthy of that perfection? Augustine says
that's the way it is in your utopia of utopias.
You are there at the start of a string of effects
turned causes. Is that where the sparrow's
strand of grass came from? And the one
before it and so on back to the claim nothing
comes from nothing? The matter that exploded
into us is still an orphan. We give it a face,
a purpose, clothe it in love so the wildly fervent
can claim to have made your acquaintance
and received your consent to slaughter folks.
Do you love that in yourself, the way you inspire
death? Or is it like death, another vision?

10.

Each day is sunny and clear; each night, rain
that need not fall on farms, highways, cars.

This great plain awakening with April grass
needs nothing more than it already has

to be what it is, what it will be. The future
does not crave our hands, our words to name

its changes and sustainings. It will awake
when we do not awake.
                         There need not be

grain waving at clouds or cattle in corrals
for you to be. Whether we are amusement,

experiment or rudiment, we are not
able to know if you tend the meadow.

A sparrow begins a nest with blades of dead
grass. She will fill it with tomorrow.

11.

prayer is our way of making you
holy
     reverse creation

we cannot say if our pain
                      this blade that scrapes
                      inside our brains
is yours or not

either way nothing changes
but ourselves

the shaman walks in an early morning field

we observe, conclude
his sandals are drenched with dew

when will it stop
               this idiot making
               of cause and consequence

12.

Prayer is one way not to starve yourself
when you have a famine of the heart
or the future is cancelled, except for pain.
Pilgrim if you can. Blood on the forehead,
blood on the knees, shoulder gouged to bone
from a cross dragged up the prescribed
stone steps in wind, raw from the salty waves,
cutting and cold, to a holy place where
a relic is encased.
                    Or wait in covers
in your final bed, and change your life
as much among the comforts of your kin,
your fate no less as you twist upwards
on a stem of agony, shrunk and waxy
gray, belated love struggling in your throat.

Gary Hyland

13.

There is nothing here. What is this place?
Not even light. Not even you. Nor sound.

Not even the soothing hum of grace.
Agony squeezed you shut. Then this, this

opening. What is this absence you feel?
An oscillation of pain made bodiless?

You would like to remember something
for context or comparison, a grid

of logic for the nonexistent ground,
a sky you could cancel with your hand.

Nothing comes. You think this might be
the perfect space for divinity

to blaze into a rose you could love.
But is this you? Were those vapours words?

14.

The first sounds will be the bottle rattle
of the milkman and the chattering sparrows.
You don't get up right away. You listen
to your mother clatter in the kitchen,
your father shaking out the paper.

The endless sun spills through the window.
You think of school. All your homework is
ready and all correct. New clothes beckon
in the closet. A playground of friends awaits.

Your father's voice, low and casual,
spreads warmth and your mother's voice responds.
One of them turns on the radio.

A voice declares eternal peace and welcomes
you to heaven. Stretching, you decide to rise.

Gary Hyland

Notes

HAMMEL: All that is known of the imaginary character Aldred Hammel is from a partially burned diary that survived a bonfire in which he incinerated his letters and manuscripts. Sociologist Wilhelm Kreuzer came into possession of the diary and decided to do an in-depth investigation of Hammel's life as part of his study of the "contributing factors to the alienation and marginalization of under-achieving North American males." Most of the details in the poems are from the diary, which covers the subject's last years from November 1998 to November 2003, a week before his death. Several of the entries contain recollections and reflections from his earlier days. He was born in Regina, Saskatchewan, Canada, in 1939 and spent most of his life there working as a file clerk for the British-American Oil Company, later Gulf Oil and presently Gulf Canada Resources.

"HAMMEL'S GEORGE SANDERS DISEASE": George Sanders was a suave English actor who starred in over 100 films including *Solomon and Sheba, Ivanhoe, All About Eve,* and *The Ghost and Mrs. Muir.* At the age of 65, in 1972, while living near Barcelona, he took an overdose of barbiturates. His suicide note read: "Dear World: I am leaving because I am bored. I am leaving you with your worries in this sweet cesspool."

"RAVEL IN AUTOMOBILE ACCIDENT" is based on *Ravel's Brain* (Bravo! May 5, 2001) a wonderfully creative documentary that looks at Ravel's final years.

"VORTAL TOMB, POULNABRONE": The breath-taking burren, south of Galway, Ireland, is named from a Gaelic word meaning "stormy place." Unspoiled since the ice age, the vast area contains a collection of megalithic tombs with relics of humans dating back 6,000 years. The "vortal tomb" near Poulnabrone is the most famous of the dolmans. The area also has numerous earthen ring forts called raths.

"MILDLY MANIC" was inspired by Alex Beam's *Gracefully Insane*, a history of McLean Hospital, a mental institution just outside of Boston, that housed the likes of John Nash, Sylvia Plath, and Robert Lowell.

"HIT AND RUNS" are written in a form I have been experimenting with for over twenty years. Thanks to Amy Caughlin for help in naming the form *sturox* after the tapered portion of a speer from classical Greece.

"STAKES IN THE RIVER" is derived from James Richardson's "Vectors: Forty-Five Aphorisms and Ten-Second Essays" that appeared in *Ploughshares* in 2000.

Acknowledgements

"His Truest Friend" is part 10 of "Excremental: Strains and Variations," which won the Newest Review satire contest in 2001.

Thanks to editor Paul Wilson for his shrewd suggestions, patience, and concerned encouragement.

I am grateful to Amy Caughlon for providing valuable feedback on several of these poems.

Special thanks for the insightful responses from members of The Poets' Combine: Byrna Barclay, Bob Currie, Judith Krause, Bruce Rice, and Paul Wilson.

Thanks always to Sharon Nichvalodoff, whose devotion makes writing possible.

Gary Hyland was born in Moose Jaw in 1940 and continues to live there. He is the founder and innovator of many institutions in Saskatchewan, including the Festival of Words, Coteau Books, and Sage Hill Writing Experience. He has published several books of poetry, including *Just off Main* (1982), *Street of Dreams* (1984), *After Atlantis* (1992), *White Crane Spreads Wings* (1996), and *The Work of Snow* (2003) which won the John V. Hicks Memorial Award sponsored by Thistledown Press. Well known as an activist and community builder, Hyland continues to be the volunteer artistic director of the extremely successful Festival of Words, which takes place each July in Moose Jaw.